ENDROLL BACK

[KANTETSU]

[HARUNA NAKAZATO]

HAAAACK
COUGH
HUFF...

GRIT

I'M SORRY...
I'M SORRY...
I'M SORRY...

SORRY...

STAGGER
TAP

ヒュオオ…
WHOOSH

...FOR EXISTING...
...IN THIS WORLD.

Loop.1 Angel

MY LITTLE
SISTER IS DEAD.

WHY DID YOU DO IT, YUUKA?
I DON'T KNOW THE REASON WHY.
AND I DIDN'T FIND A NOTE.

BUT...
SHE WAS BULLIED, WASN'T SHE?
EVEN THOUGH SHE WAS ONE OF THE POPULAR KIDS AS A FIRST YEAR.

I HEARD THAT SHE SLEPT WITH A BUNCH OF OLDER STUDENTS.
AND I HEARD THAT SHE HUMILIATED HER FRIENDS TO GET A SPOT IN THE CLUB.
!

I'M SURE...

...THAT GIRL IS A FRIEND OF YUUKA'S.

*YUUKA MAMIYA'S FUNERAL CEREMONY

YOU HAVE TO BE A REAL WEAKLING, AND SICK IN THE HEAD, TO DO THAT.

YOU CAN'T SAY THAT AT A TIME LIKE THIS.
...

BUT I'M RIGHT, AREN'T I?

DAMN, I WISH I'D SCREWED HER ONE LAST TIME BEFORE SHE KILLED HERSELF.

!!

WHOOSH

STOP!!
!
!
SLAM

WHY...? WHY DO ASSHOLES LIKE THIS GET TO LIVE?

AND YUUKA DOESN'T...?

I'M SORRY WE CAN'T LIVE TOGETHER.

I REALLY, ABSOLUTELY HAVE TO MOVE. WILL YOU BE ALRIGHT EVEN THOUGH I'M LEAVING?
I'LL BE FINE. DON'T WORRY.

I'M A REALLY HAPPY GIRL NOW.

THAT'S WHY...
SHE STILL HAD HER WHOLE LIFE AHEAD OF HER.

STARTING TODAY, WE WILL INVESTIGATE ANY POTENTIAL INSTANCES OF ANYONE BULLYING HER.
THAT WON'T BE NECESSARY.

I'VE ALREADY HEARD MORE THAN ENOUGH TODAY. IT'S YOUR FAULT...!!

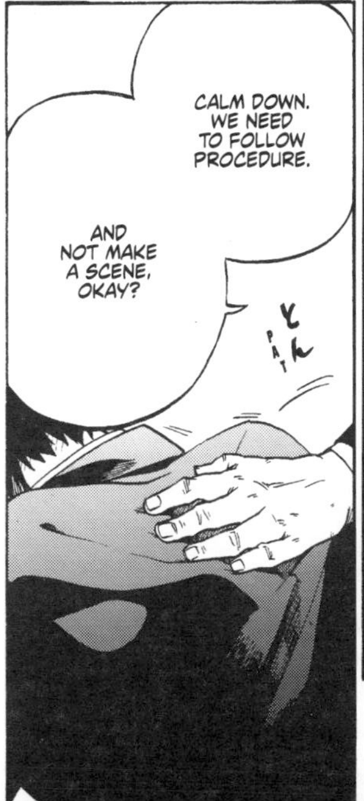
CALM DOWN. WE NEED TO FOLLOW PROCEDURE.
AND NOT MAKE A SCENE, OKAY?
PAT

IT'S SO OBVIOUS THAT IT'S THEIR FAULT.
GRIT

ARE...

ARE YOU YUUKA'S BROTHER?
I AM.

MY NAME IS ITSUKI TOJIMA.

COULD WE TALK FOR A MINUTE?

HERE.

T-THANK YOU...

WHAT DID YOU WANT TO TELL ME?

IT'S...
ABOUT YUUKA.

IF YOU'RE GOING TO TELL ME THAT SHE WAS BULLIED, I ALREADY KNOW THAT.
THE ONES THAT DID IT ARE THOSE BOYS OVER THERE.

Y-YEAH...

SQUEEZE

AND EVEN THOUGH I KNEW ABOUT IT, I DIDN'T DO A THING TO STOP IT...
I'M SO SORRY.

WHEN I WAS 15, OUR FATHER WAS ARRESTED.

HE WAS A PIECE OF SHIT.
AFTER THEY FIRED HIM, HE JUST DRANK DAY AFTER DAY.
AND HE HIT WHOEVER HE FELT LIKE.

UNTIL HE ENDED UP GETTING SENT TO JAIL FOR KILLING SOMEONE.
BECAUSE OF HIM OUR FAMILY HAD A BAD REPUTATION IN THE NEIGHBOR-HOOD AND AT SCHOOL.
I HEARD THAT MR. MAMIYA IS A MURDERER.

I HEARD THAT HE DIDN'T HAVE A JOB.
THEY SAY THAT THEY'VE ARRESTED HIS DAD.
DON'T TALK TO THEM. THEY MIGHT KILL YOU.
I HEARD THAT HIS WIFE ENDED UP HURT TOO.
WHAT A DAN-GEROUS FAMILY.
THE KIDS OF A KILLER.

IT WAS A LI-VING HELL.

IT WASN'T BECAU-SE OUR FATHER WAS A DISGRACE, BUT BECAUSE...
THEY SAW US AS THE CHILDREN OF A KILLER.

THAT'S WHY I WORKED MYSELF TO THE BONE, SO THAT THEY WOULDN'T LOOK DOWN ON US.
I'LL NEVER FORGIVE THOSE THAT RUINED OUR LIVES.
MORE THAN ANYTHING IN THE WORLD, I WANTED TO SPARE YUUKA FROM THAT SHITTY LIFE.

THAT'S WHY I WORKED PART-TIME JOBS...
...FINISHED HIGH SCHOOL, AND STARTED WORKING.
I MADE IT SO THAT YUUKA WOULD GO TO A SCHOOL THAT WAS FAR AWAY.

WHEN SHE STARTED AT YOUR SCHOOL, NO ONE KNEW ABOUT WHAT HAD HAPPENED WITH OUR FATHER.
SHE WAS ABLE TO MAKE FRIENDS, JOIN A CLUB. SHE STARTED LAUGHING AGAIN, JUST LIKE SHE USED TO.
I HAD FINALLY DONE IT. I WAS ABLE TO SEE YUUKA SMILE AGAIN.
HER LIFE WAS JUST BEGINNING...

I DON'T UNDERSTAND WHY THOSE KIDS GET TO LAUGH AND YUUKA DOESN'T.

...

UMM...

THE TRUTH IS...
VRRRRR

OH, SORRY...
VRRR

ス
SWIPE

キョロキョロ
GLANCE GLANCE
?

RISE
WHAT'S GOING ON?
S-SO-RRY...

I HAVE TO GO.
W-WHAT?!

WHAT'S WITH HIM?

FLASH

UGH...
OOH...
UGH...
THEY'RE THE KILLER'S KIDS!

I'M SORRY, BROTHER...

WHY ARE YOU SAYING SORRY? YOU DIDN'T DO ANYTHING WRONG.
IT'S MY FAULT THAT...
IT'S OK. THIS IS NOTHING.
SO DON'T WORRY. YOU CAN COUNT ON ME. I'LL ALWAYS BE THERE FOR YOU.

...
YOU SHOULD BE HAPPY, SO JUST LEAVE THESE BAD THINGS TO ME.
WOW, EVERYTHING'S COVERED IN SAND.
WE'LL HAVE TO THROW IT ALL AWAY.
NO!
...

BUT YOUR PENCIL CASE...
POOF
NOPE!
YOUR HANDKER-CHIEF...
POOF
NOPE!
YOUR KEYCHAIN...
POOF
NOPE!
LISTEN...
YOU GAVE ME ALL OF THOSE THINGS.
BUT THEY'RE NOT CUTE. THEY'RE BOY THINGS.
ACTUALLY, SHE STOLE THEM FROM ME.
SHAKE ふる
SHAKE ふる
I WANT TO HAVE THE SAME THINGS AS YOU.

THAT'S WHY I DON'T CARE IF THEY'RE UGLY. I WANT TO SHARE THEM WITH YOU. AND I'LL GET STRONGER TOO AND NOT CRY.
I WANT BOTH OF US TO BE HAPPY.
...
YOU'RE RIGHT...
PAT
WE'LL BOTH BE HAPPY TOGETHER.
I PROMISE.
WE'LL BOTH BE HAPPY TOGETHER.

I PROMISED HER THAT...

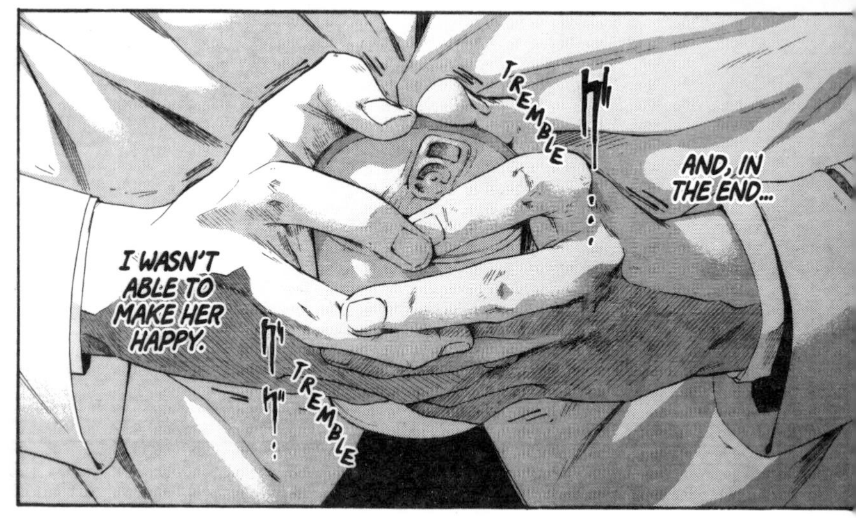
TREMBLE
AND, IN THE END...
I WASN'T ABLE TO MAKE HER HAPPY.
TREMBLE

I COULDN'T DO A THING...
YUUKA...

OH, POOR YOU.
FLUTTER

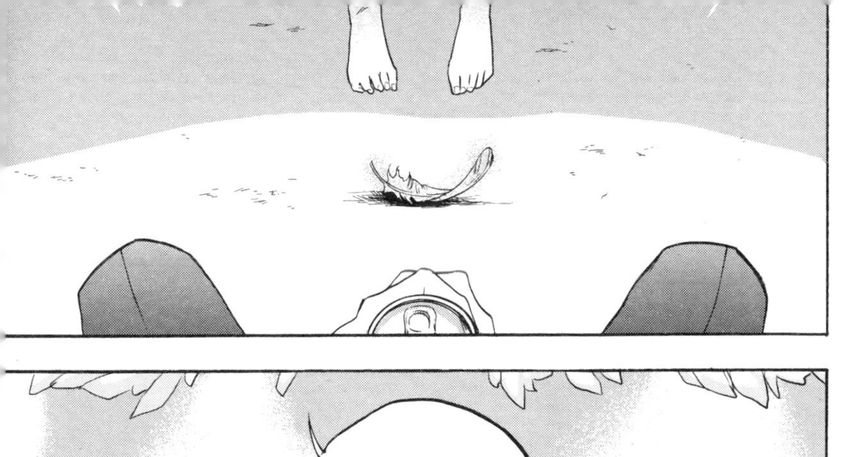

HEY...

DO YOU WANT ME TO GIVE YOU ANOTHER CHANCE?

WHAT?!

YOU HAVE TO KILL YUUKA MAMIYA'S KILLER.
IF YOU DO THAT, I'LL BRING HER BACK TO LIFE.

IF YOU WANT YOUR LITTLE SISTER TO LIVE AGAIN, LET'S MAKE A PACT!
IF YOU DO EVERYTHING I SAY AND FOLLOW ALL OF MY RULES TO THE LETTER, YOU CAN CHANGE THIS REALITY.
YOUR SISTER'S DEATH WILL BE HISTORY.

ARE YOU WILLING TO RISK YOUR LIFE FOR YOUR SISTER, ASAHARU MAMIYA?
OR...

...DO YOU WANT TO LIVE WITH ALL THAT REGRET?
I DON'T UNDERSTAND WHAT SHE'S TELLING ME.
BRING MY SISTER BACK TO LIFE? RISK MY OWN LIFE?
AM I DREAMING?
WHAT DO YOU SAY, ASAHARU MAMIYA?

NO... I DON'T CARE IF THIS IS A DREAM OR AN ILLUSION.

GRIT
IF I CAN KILL THEM...

IF I CAN MAKE YUUKA HAPPY, I...

PACT SEALED!
SNAP
CRACK

CRACK
CRACK
CRACK
CRACK
?!
CRASH

HEY...
WHOOSH

LET THE GAMES BEGIN.

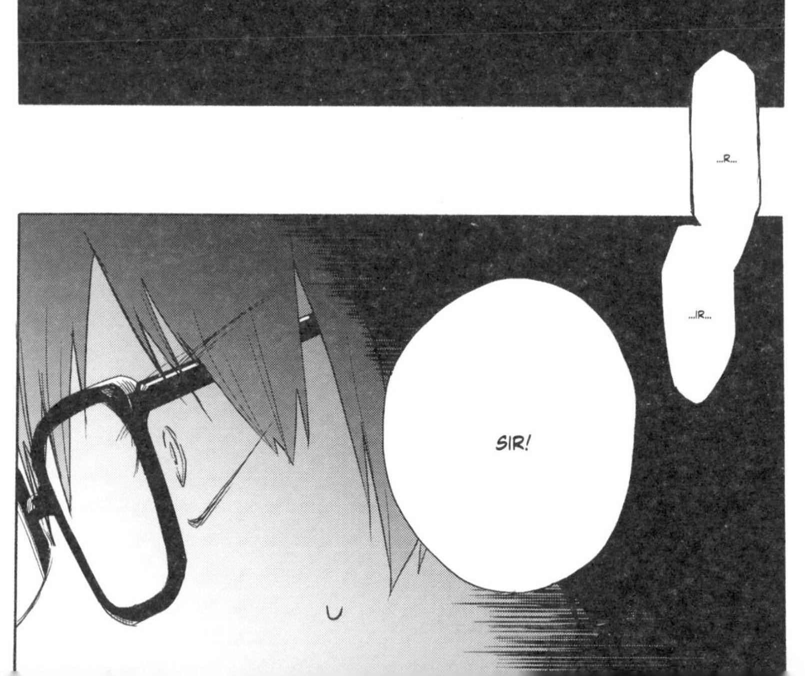
...R...
...IR...
SIR!

NERVOUS?
?!

WHERE AM I?
AND WHO IS THIS WOMAN?

HUH?!
GRAB
GRAB

PLEASE, COME IN. DON'T BE SHY.

REMEMBER THAT YOU'RE GOING TO BE THEIR SUBSTITUTE TEACHER FOR THE NEXT THREE MONTHS.
PUSH
グイッ
WHAT?
QUIET, EVERYONE.

I'VE SEEN THEM BEFORE.
LIKE I TOLD YOU ALL BEFORE, MR. FUKUDA IS IN THE HOSPITAL DUE TO HIS ILLNESS.
THAT'S WHY, UNTIL HE RETURNS TO OUR SCHOOL...
STARTING TODAY, MR. HIYOSHI WILL TAKE OVER THE CLASS.
I'M SURE THAT THEY'RE THE ONES FROM THE FUNERAL. YUUKA'S CLASSMATES.
IF THAT'S THE CASE, THEN THIS IS...
...TATEOKA ACADEMY.

WELL, WHY DON'T YOU INTRODUCE YOURSELF?
OH, RIGHT...
RAISE
!!

YAWN
SCRATCH
SCRATCH
THAT'S...

YOU HAVE TO KILL YUUKA MAMIYA'S KILLER.

IF YOU DO THAT, I'LL BRING HER BACK TO LIFE.
THAT'S WHAT I HAVE TO DO.

THIS...
SIR?
TAP
TAP
TAP
REACH
...
?
GRAB
CLACK

ALL THIS WILL BE OVER IF I KILL YOU.

REACH
HUH? WHAT ARE YOU DOING?!
EH? WAIT...
CLICK CLICK CLICK
A BOX CUTTER!

ピタ…
IT'S FUNNY WATCHING YOU GO FOR IT RIGHT FROM THE JUMP...
...BUT THIS IS THE FIRST TIME I'VE SEEN AN IDIOT NOT STOP TO THINK ABOUT THINGS.
WHY HAVE YOU APPEARED?
IT'S JUST THAT...
...I SAID I NEEDED TO EXPLAIN THE RULES TO YOU, DIDN'T I? HOW THE GAME IS PLAYED...
WHOOSH

SLASH
SPLURT

IF I KILL HER KI-LLER...
...THIS ALL ENDS, RIGHT?
SLAM
WHAT AN EASY GAME.

ASAHARU...

...YOU'RE SUCH AN IDIOT.
CRACK

CRASH

BOOM

WHOOSH
!!

WHAT HAPPENED?
WHAT A SHAME...

YOU'LL HAVE TO START ALL OVER AGAIN.
BADUMP
AND WITH A PENALTY TOO.
SMIRK

U-UGH...
THROB
SLAM
CLACK

WHAT'S HAPPENING TO ME?! ALL OF A SUDDEN MY BODY IS...!

YOU'VE JUST LOST 10 YEARS OF YOUR LIFESPAN.

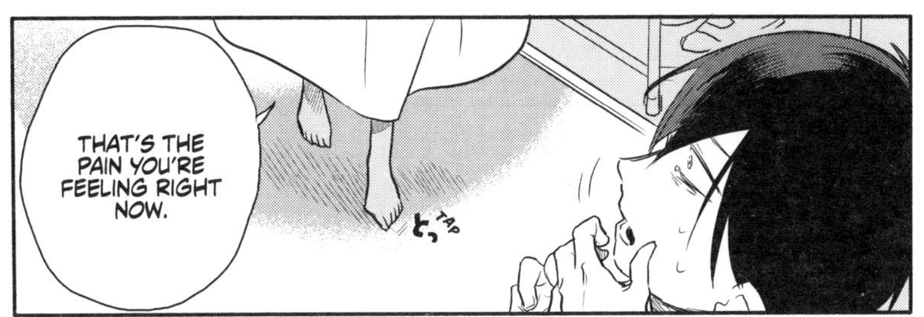
THAT'S THE PAIN YOU'RE FEELING RIGHT NOW.
TAP

YOUR INTERNAL ORGANS JUST FELT THE CONSEQUENCES OF AGING 10 YEARS.
10 YEARS OF MY LIFE...?

HOW MANY ARE LEFT?

DON'T LOOK AT ME. I'M NOT GOING TO TELL YOU.
WHAT?!

THIS IS SO MUCH MORE EXCITING IF YOU DON'T KNOW HOW MANY YOU HAVE LEFT.
I LOVE A GOOD TWIST.

DON'T WORRY. ALL YOU HAVE TO DO IS NOT MESS UP.

BUT, ISN'T HE THE ONE RESPONSIBLE?
THAT'S THE KID THAT BULLIED YUUKA!
ARE YOU SURE THAT'S TRUE?
HUH?

MAYBE THE FACT THAT THE BOY IS RESPONSIBLE FOR THE DEATH OF YUUKA MAMIYA IS ALL IN YOUR HEAD?
POINT
YOU NEED TO DISTINGUISH BETWEEN WHAT'S TRUE AND WHAT'S FALSE, ASAHARU MAMIYA.
DON'T ACT BASED ON YOUR IMAGINATION AND PREJUDICES.

FLAP
YOU NEED TO BE ABLE TO JUDGE IT FOR YOURSELF.
OTHERWISE...

...YOU WILL
DIE.

ENDROLL BACK

OTHERWISE...
YOU WILL DIE.
Loop.2 Friends

WOAH, YOU
SCARED?

SHUT UP.
I TOLD YOU THAT I'M READY TO RISK WHATEVER IT TAKES, INCLUDING MY LIFE.

HA, HA. WHAT A RELIEF.

IF SOMETHING SO SIMPLE HAD SCARED YOU...
...THIS WOULD HAVE BEEN NO FUN AT ALL.

WELL, GO ON WITH EXPLAINING THE RULES.

SIR, PLEASE, INTRODUCE YOURSELF.

FROM NOW ON, I'LL BE YOUR TEACHER.
MY NAME IS ASAHARU HIYOSHI.

I HOPE WE'LL ALL GET ALONG DURING THESE NEXT THREE MONTHS.

RULE 1: IN THIS WORLD, YOU ARE NOT ASAHARU MAMIYA. YOU ARE ROOM 2B'S NEW TEACHER, ASAHARU HIYOSHI.
THANK YOU.

WHILE WE WAIT FOR MR. FUKUDA TO RETURN...
...MR. HIYOSHI WILL BE IN CHARGE OF THE CLASS.

RULE 2: YOU HAVE FROM SEPTEMBER 1ST TO MIDNIGHT DECEMBER 23RD.

MR. HIYOSHI WILL TEACH JAPANESE HISTORY.
SO HE WILL ALSO COVER FOR MR. FUKUDA IN THAT CLASS.
YOU NEED TO FIND WHO IN THE CLASS IS THE CULPRIT...

...AND KILL THEM.

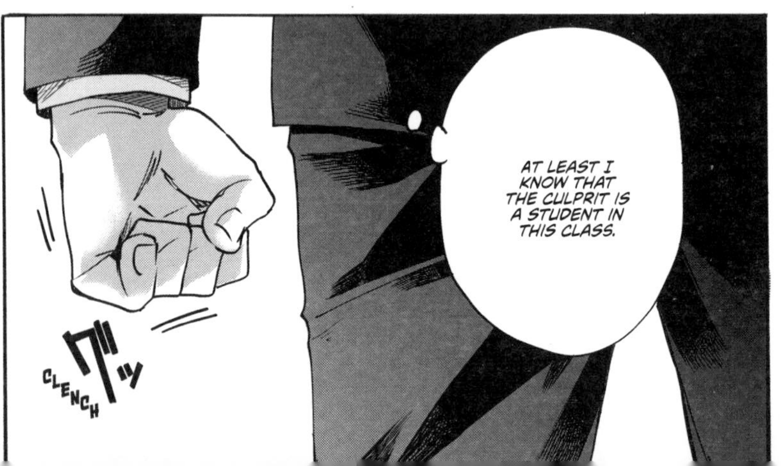
AT LEAST I KNOW THAT THE CULPRIT IS A STUDENT IN THIS CLASS.
CLENCH

RULE 3: IF YOU KILL THE CULPRIT, YUUKA MAMIYA WILL COME BACK TO LIFE.
HOWEVER...

IF YOU CHOOSE INCORRECTLY...

RULE 4: YOU'LL HAVE TO START ALL OVER AGAIN FROM SEPTEMBER 1ST, AND YOU WILL LOSE 10 YEARS OF YOUR LIFESPAN AS A PENALTY.
RULE 5: BUT YOU WILL NEVER KNOW HOW MANY YEARS OF LIFE YOU HAVE LEFT.

SHIT...
I HAVE NO IDEA HOW MANY TIMES I CAN START OVER AGAIN.
FOR NOW, THAT'S THE ONLY INFORMATION I CAN COUNT ON.
SCRAPE
?

AND ALSO...

RIGHT NOW, YOU'RE IN THE PAST.
す
SLIDE
YU...

OF COURSE...

YUUKA MAMIYA EXISTS HERE.
SORRY FOR BEING LATE.

YUUKA...
SHE'S REALLY ALIVE.
HM.

YOU'RE LATE AGAIN, MAMIYA...
YOU SHOULD BE MORE CAREFUL.
す
TURN

MR. HIYOSHI?
TAP
TAP
!!
GRAB

ARE YOU OK, YUUKA?!
UMM
?!

WHY DO YOU HAVE THAT BANDAGE ON?
WHO HURT YOU?

HUH?
W-WHAT'S GOING ON?

!
チラ…
GLANCE

YOUR LEG IS HURT TOO! HAVE YOU NOTICED?
CROUCH
!

!!
SLAM
PLEASE STOP! WHO ARE YOU?
WHAT DO YOU MEAN...? I'M...

!

ハァ…
SIGH

RULE 6: YOU CANNOT INTERFERE WITH THIS WORLD AS ASAHARU MAMIYA, SO BE CAREFUL.

MR. HIYOSHI...?

...

TEACHERS' ROOM
I'M SO SORRY.

JUST...
BE CAREFUL WITH HOW YOU INTERACT WITH THE STUDENTS, OK?
LATELY, ANY LITTLE THING TURNS INTO A PROBLEM.

SHE DEFINITELY SEES YOU AS A REAL WEIRDO.
QUIT YOUR YAPPING.

SO... GOOD, WE'VE FINISHED WITH EVERYTHING RELATED TO MR. FUKUDA.
DO YOU NEED ME TO GIVE YOU A TOUR OF THE SCHOOL?

DON'T WORRY. I HAVE A BIT OF TIME BEFORE THE NEXT CLASS, SO I WAS THINKING ABOUT WALKING AROUND THE SCHOOL.
IT'LL BE EASIER IF I ACT ALONE.

THAT'S FINE. AFTER ALL, IT'S NOT SUCH A BIG PLACE.
IS THERE ANYTHING YOU'D LIKE TO ASK ME?
...

HAVE THERE BEEN ANY CASES OF BULLYING...
IN THE CLASS?

WHY ARE YOU ASKING ABOUT THAT?

IT'S JUST THAT MAMIYA WAS HURT...

グッ
GRIP
YUU...

THERE'S NO REASON TO WORRY ABOUT HER.
IT'S NATURAL TO GET A BIT HURT SOMETIMES IN THE BASKETBALL CLUB.
EVERYONE IN THAT CLASS IS AN EXCELLENT STUDENT.
TATEOKA ACADEMY

I SEE...

SO THERE'S NO BULLYING AT SCHOOL...
THAT'S OBVIOUSLY A LIE.

SO? YOU THINK YOU'LL BE ABLE TO FIND THE CULPRIT?
YOU'RE UNBEARABLE.

I STILL CAN'T MAKE ANY CONCLUSIONS.
I KNOW THAT YOU HAVEN'T EXACTLY MADE THE BEST FIRST IMPRESSION WITH THE STUDENTS...
...

I NEED TO COLLECT INFORMATION AND KILL THE STUDENT THAT I THINK IS RESPONSIBLE.
...

HEY...
WHAT HAPPENS IF I DON'T KILL ANYONE WITHIN THE TIME LIMIT?

THE GAME ENDS.
YOU'LL GET A PENALTY EQUAL TO HOW MANY TIMES YOU CHOSE INCORRECTLY.
I SEE.

IT DOESN'T MAKE MUCH SENSE FOR ME TO PROTECT YUUKA.
AH, OF COURSE. REMEMBER THAT THE OBJECTIVE IS TO FIND AND KILL THE ONE RESPONSIBLE FOR HER DEATH.
NOT TO STOP HER DEATH.

DON'T OVERTHINK IT.
SMACK
I THINK THE BEST THING TO DO WOULD BE TO CONCENTRATE ON FINDING THE CULPRIT.
I'VE GIVEN YOU A FEW ABILITIES TO HELP WITH THAT.
HA, ABILITIES...

THAT'S ALL FOR TODAY.
I HAVE ONE FINAL SPECIAL SOMETHING FOR YOU.
FLASH
!

FLASH
WHAT IS THIS?
ABILITIES, OR, RATHER, SPECIAL TALENTS.
ALL GAMES HAVE THEM, DON'T THEY?

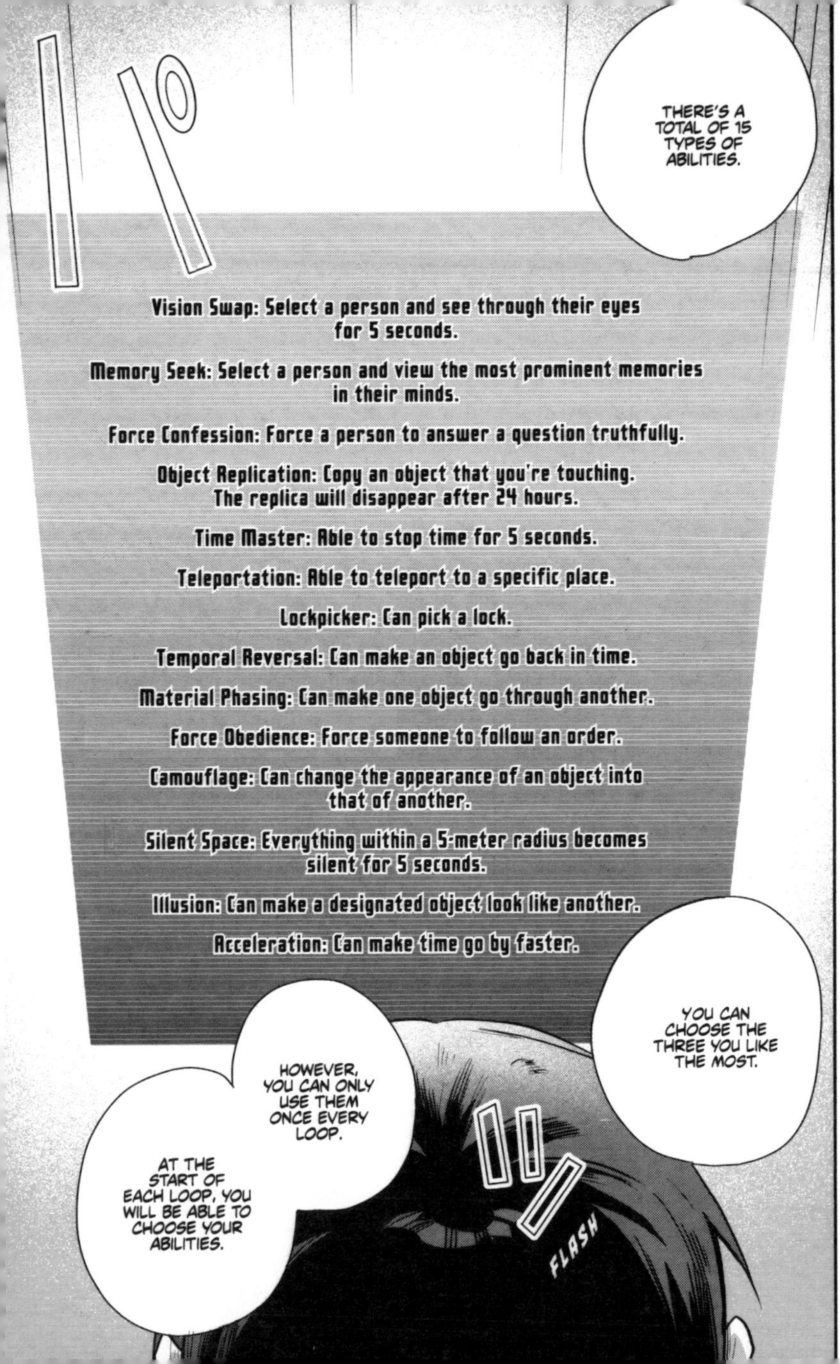

THERE'S A TOTAL OF 15 TYPES OF ABILITIES.

Vision Swap: Select a person and see through their eyes for 5 seconds.

Memory Seek: Select a person and view the most prominent memories in their minds.

Force Confession: Force a person to answer a question truthfully.

Object Replication: Copy an object that you're touching. The replica will disappear after 24 hours.

Time Master: Able to stop time for 5 seconds.

Teleportation: Able to teleport to a specific place.

Lockpicker: Can pick a lock.

Temporal Reversal: Can make an object go back in time.

Material Phasing: Can make one object go through another.

Force Obedience: Force someone to follow an order.

Camouflage: Can change the appearance of an object into that of another.

Silent Space: Everything within a 5-meter radius becomes silent for 5 seconds.

Illusion: Can make a designated object look like another.

Acceleration: Can make time go by faster.

YOU CAN CHOOSE THE THREE YOU LIKE THE MOST.

HOWEVER, YOU CAN ONLY USE THEM ONCE EVERY LOOP.

AT THE START OF EACH LOOP, YOU WILL BE ABLE TO CHOOSE YOUR ABILITIES.

FLASH

STOP TIME, MANIPULATE MEMORIES, VISION SWAP...
THERE'S ALL KINDS OF ABILITIES.
THAT'S QUITE GENEROUS OF YOU.

I TOLD YOU. I ENJOY A GOOD SHOW.

COME ON, CHOOSE WHATEVER YOU WANT.

I WON'T BE ABLE TO CHANGE MY ABILITIES UNTIL THE NEXT LOOP.
I NEED TO BE SMART ABOUT THIS.
...
Vision Swap: Select a perso d see through
SWIPE
Memory Seek: Select a pe son and
Force Confession: For e a person to answer

I CHOOSE THESE THREE.
YOU DON'T WANT TELEPORTATION?
WHERE DO YOU THINK I'D BE ABLE TO USE IT?

I'VE CHOSEN ABILITIES THAT WILL LET ME COLLECT INFOR-MATION...
BUT I CAN ONLY USE THEM ONCE, SO I NEED TO BE CAREFUL WITH THEM.
TEACHER!

WHAT ARE YOU DOING...
...HERE?

OH, YOU'RE...
I'M HIMENO SAEKI.

THIS GIRL WAS CRYING THE DAY OF THE FUNERAL.

I WAS JUST FAMILIARIZING MYSELF WITH THE SCHOOL.
AND WHAT ARE YOU DOING HERE? I'D IMAGINE YOU HAVE SCIENCE DURING FIRST PERIOD.
I CAME HERE TO LOOK FOR SOMETHING I FORGOT.
AND WHEN I SAW YOU, I THOUGHT I'D TALK TO YOU.

I THOUGHT TO MYSELF, WHAT COULD HAVE BEEN GOING THROUGH HIS MIND WHEN HE WENT TO HUG YUUKA?
HUH?!

I DIDN'T HUG HER! I WAS JUST WORRIED BECAUSE SHE WAS HURT.
UMM...

HEE HEE
THAT'S REALLY NICE OF YOU.

IT'S NORMAL. GO ON, GET TO CLASS.
I'M GOOOOOING.
TURN

ぴ
た
PAUSE
OH...

BECAUSE I'M THE CLASS REPRESENTATIVE, PLEASE FEEL FREE TO ASK ME ANY QUESTIONS.

NICE TO MEET YOU, MR. HIYOSHI.

SHE DOESN'T SEEM LIKE A BAD PERSON.

TODAY WE WILL GO UP TO HERE.

WHOOSH
THIS BEING A TEACHER THING COMES SO NATURALLY TO YOU. I THOUGHT YOU'D STRUGGLE A BIT.

IT'S BECAUSE I WAS AN HONOR STUDENT.

TEACHERS' ROOM
ガラッ
SLIDE

CREAK
ギッ

IT'S WEIRD TO NOT INTERACT WITH YUUKA.
I'LL EAT QUICKLY SO I CAN GO LOOK FOR CLUES IN THE CLASSROOM.

WOW, YOU BROUGHT YOUR OWN FOOD TOO. DID YOU MAKE IT YOURSELF?
すっ
WAVE
HUH? OH, YES...

THAT'S INCREDIBLE. YOU'RE SO YOUNG. DO YOU LIVE ALONE?
YES. I MOVED HERE THIS PAST SPRING.

LOOKS LIKE THIS IS GOING TO TAKE A WHILE.
BUT I CAN'T DO ANYTHING ABOUT IT, BECAUSE I'M NEW HERE...

ヒュッ
WHOOSH
KYAH!
SPLAT

OH, SORRY ABOUT THAT. THE BALL SLIPPED.

YOU'RE SO CLUMSY, NAMI.

...

THIS IS OUR SPOT. DO US A FAVOR AND MOVE.
I-I'M SORRY. I'LL LEAVE NOW.

HURRY UP!

STEP
す
!

...

COME ON, AKANE. LET'S EAT ALREADY.
Y-YEAH...

MURMUR
MURMUR
MURMUR

DONE...
OOF...
IS IT OK FOR YOU TO BE DOING THIS?
PLOP

I DON'T HAVE A CHOICE. THE NEW GUY CAN'T REFUSE ANYTHING ASKED OF HIM.
UMM...
CAN I ASK YOU TO ORGANIZE THE RECORDS IN THIS ROOM...?
IF I REFUSE TO DO IT, THEY CAN LABEL ME AS INSOLENT, AND THAT WOULD MAKE THINGS HARDER FOR ME.
BEING THE NEW GUY IS HARD NO MATTER WHERE YOU ARE...

I SHOULD HURRY AND GO SEE YUUKA.

HUH?

?

THAT GIRL...
THAT'S YUUKA'S FRIEND...

I CAN'T SEE WHAT'S HAPPENING VERY WELL...
I HAVE NO OTHER OPTION.

TELL ME, HOW DO I USE MY ABILITIES?
YOU ONLY NEED TO WISH TO DO SO.

YOU SURE?
IT DOESN'T MAKE SENSE TO BE TOO CAUTIOUS.

Sigh

VISION SWAP
TARGET: AKANE SHIMIZU

WHOOSH

TREMBLE
ふる
TREMBLE
ふる
バッ
WHOOSH

HUH?

Organic Waste

HOW DID SHE KNOW I WAS WATCHING HER?
BECAUSE THE VISION SWAP SWITCHES WHAT YOU'RE BOTH SEEING.
WHILE YOU WERE LOOKING THROUGH HER EYES, SHE COULD SEE THAT YOU WERE LOOKING AT HER.
IN OTHER WORDS, SHE JUST SAW HER OWN BACK.

IT HAS THAT DRAWBACK?!
SHE GAVE ME AN AWFUL EXPLANATION!

EITHER WAY...

THOSE TENNIS SHOES...

SLIDE
ガラッ
Burnable Waste
Organic Waste

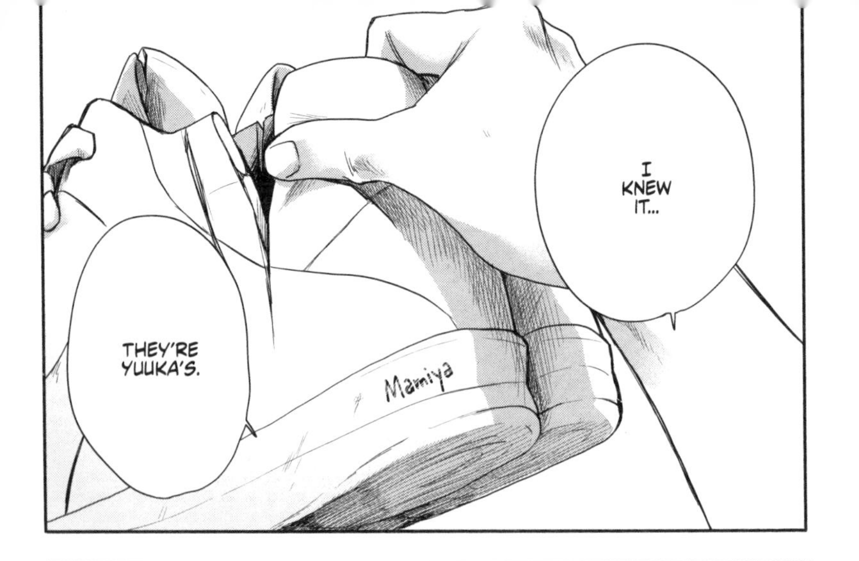
I KNEW IT...
THEY'RE YUUKA'S.
Mamiya

THOSE...

OH!
!

FLOP
LOOKING FOR THESE?
...

AKANE SHIMIZU FROM OUR CLASS AND...
...I THINK IT WAS SOMEONE FROM THE BASKETBALL TEAM...
WAIT! THIS IS BULLYING!

YOU'RE WRONG. THE NEW FAD IS HIDING PEOPLE'S THINGS.
THEY'RE JUST PLAYING AROUND.

THEY WOULDN'T DO SOMETHING LIKE THAT IF THEY WERE JUST PLAYING AROUND.
WHY DID THEY DO IT?

IF YOU TELL ME THE REASON...
I'M FINE. DON'T WORRY ABOUT IT.

PLEASE DON'T BUTT INTO THIS.

I CAN'T IGNORE IT.
REACH
すっ

YOU COULD TELL ME THE DETAILS IN SOME...

PLEASE STOP BOTHERING ME. DON'T TALK TO ME ANYMORE.

...

HEY, MR. HIYOSHI.

WHAT ARE YOU DOING?
OH, SAEKI...

WOW, THAT'S QUITE A MESS. WHAT WERE YOU DOING?
THEY HAD THROWN MAMIYA'S TENNIS SHOES AWAY.

I SAW SHIMIZU FROM OUR CLASS AND TWO OTHER GIRLS WHEN THEY WERE THROWN AWAY.
AH, THEY MUST BE FROM THE BASKETBALL TEAM.

ARE THEY BULLYING MAMIYA?

YES, BECAUSE OF THE BASKETBALL CLUB.
WHAT HAPPENED?

PLEASE...
...TELL ME WHAT YOU KNOW.

ふぅ… SIGH
ALRIGHT, BUT IT'S ONLY THINGS THAT I'VE HEARD.

BEFORE THE GAME LAST SUMMER, SOMEONE RUINED THE TENNIS SHOES OF THE THIRD-YEAR GIRLS.
AND THEY ACCUSED MAMIYA OF DOING IT.

Organic Waste
mable Waste
WHY HER?
BECAUSE OUR BASKETBALL TEAM ISN'T VERY GOOD AND IT WAS THE LAST MATCH OF THE YEAR THAT THE THIRD YEARS WOULD BE ABLE TO PLAY IN.
BUT YUUKA WAS NOTICEABLY BETTER THAN EVERYONE ELSE.

AND THEY SAID SHE WASN'T HAPPY ABOUT SOMEONE WORSE THAN HER HAVING A REGULAR SPOT ON THE TEAM...
THAT'S WHY SHE DID THAT PRANK.
AT LEAST, THAT'S WHAT I HEARD.

SHE WOULD NEVER DO SOMETHING LIKE THAT.
ぐ…
CLENCH

AKANE WAS A CLOSE FRIEND OF YUUKA BACK THEN.

BUT EVER SINCE THAT INCIDENT...
...YUUKA STARTED AVOIDING ME TOO.
I UNDERSTAND. THANK YOU.

ALL THIS...

WHY ARE YOU SO INTERESTED IN YUUKA?
I THINK THE REASON IS OBVIOUS.

I'M JUST WORRIED.
YOU REALLY ARE WEIRD.

キュ
SQUEAK
キュ
SQUEAK
BOUNCE
BOUNCE

BAM
どッ

YUUKA WOULD NEVER HURT ANYONE FOR PERSONAL REASONS.
THEY MUST HAVE FRAMED HER.
CLENCH
BAM

IT'S QUITE OBVIOUS.

YUUKA AND AKANE SHIMIZU ARE THE ONLY STUDENTS IN ROOM 2B THAT ARE IN THE BASKETBALL CLUB.

GOOD MORNING!
RECORDS

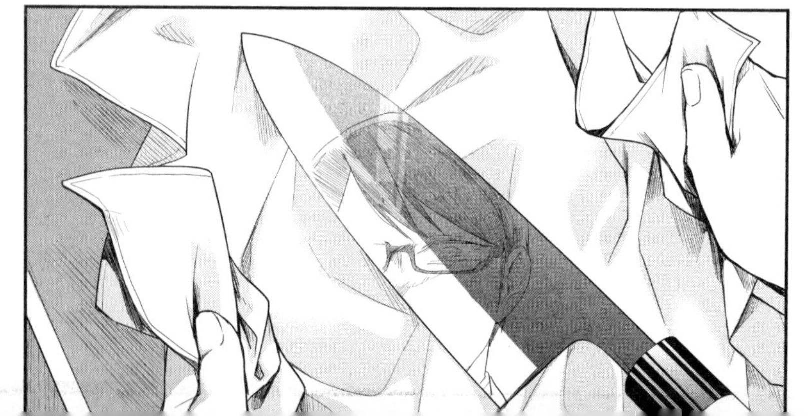

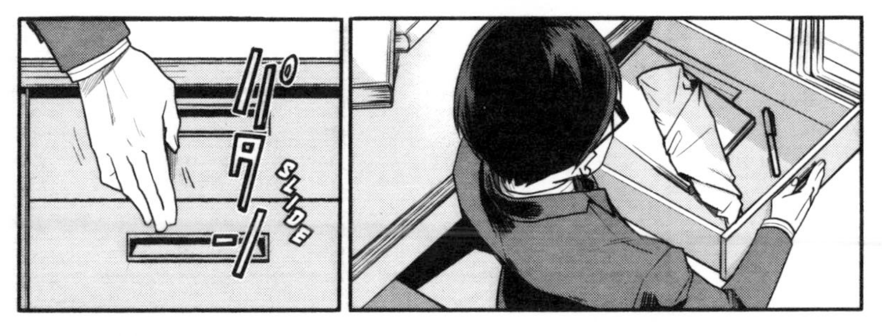
SLIDE

GOOD MORNING, SHIMIZU.
!

GO--
GOOD MORNING, MR. HIYOSHI.

CAN I HELP YOU?

THERE'S SOMETHING I'D LIKE TO ASK YOU.
SMILE

COULD YOU PLEASE COME WITH ME?

I HAVE THINGS TO DO.
ズッ
BLOCK
!

IT'LL BE QUICK.
IF YOU SAY SO...

ALRIGHT...

RECORDS
WHAT HAPPENED YESTERDAY?

WHAT ARE YOU TALKING ABOUT?

YOU THREW AWAY MAMIYA'S TENNIS SHOES, DIDN'T YOU?
AND YOU ALSO CUT THEM UP.

YOU'RE WRONG. IT WAS JUST A COINCIDENCE THAT THEY WERE IN THE BAG OF TRASH.

THEN WHY DID YOU RUN AWAY?

I DIDN'T RUN AWAY.
I WAS GOING TO TELL A SCHOOL COUNSELOR ABOUT IT.
ボリボリ
SCRATCH SCRATCH

THIS IS A WASTE OF TIME. IT'LL BE FASTER IF I JUST LOOK DIRECTLY INTO YOUR MEMORIES.
?
す
HOVER

WHAT...?
BLINK
WHAT ARE YOU DOING...?
MEMORY SEEK
VIEW THE MEMORIES RELATED TO YUUKA

FLASH
FLASH

YUUKA MAMIYA SHOULD SUFFER! SHE DESERVES TO BE PUNISHED.
FLASH

DAMN... THEY'RE TOO VAGUE. THIS DOESN'T HELP ME AT ALL.
SLIDE
W-WHAT ARE YOU DOING...?
YOU WERE JEALOUS OF MAMIYA, WEREN'T YOU?
HUH?

THAT'S WHY YOU WANTED HER TO SUFFER, RIGHT?
I DIDN'T...

THAT'S WHY YOU CUT UP THE TENNIS SHOES DURING THE GAME AND FRAMED HER!
I DIDN'T DO THAT!!
IT'S USELESS TO ASK HER ABOUT IT.
I HAVE TO MAKE HER TALK.
CLENCH

FORCE CONFESSION
ANSWER.
WERE YOU THE ONE THAT CUT UP THE TENNIS SHOES?

FLASH

YES...
IT WAS ME.

THAT'S IT.
GASP
HUH...?
I...

N-NO!!

YOU JUST CONFESSED.
I DIDN'T...
ガタッ
BANG

I'M TIRED OF HEARING EXCUSES.
すっ
STAND
?
する
GLINT
HUH...?
WHAT'S THAT?
REVEAL

H-HEL--
ガタン
CRASH
ぐぐ…
SQUEEZE

IT'S OVER...
MMHPH
SCRATCH...

WHAT'S THE MATTER?

NOW YOU'RE SCARED?

SHUT UP.

HOW DISAPPOINTING.
I DIDN'T THINK YOU'D BE SO WEAK.
SHUT THE HELL UP!
WHY AM I HESITATING?
I'VE ALREADY KILLED ONE BEFORE.

I JUST NEED TO STAB HER LIKE I DID LAST TIME.
BUT STILL...

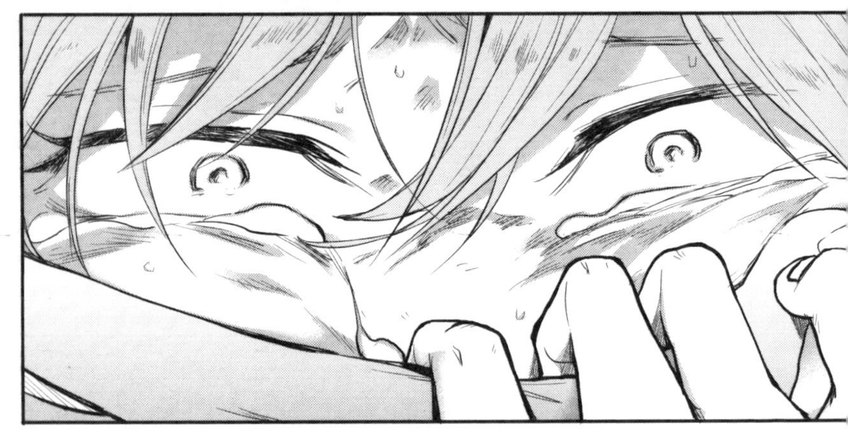

YOU'RE SCARED, AREN'T YOU?

I GET IT NOW... BACK THEN I HAD STOPPED TIME.
IT'S THE FIRST TIME YOU'RE SEEING THE TERROR IN THE EYES OF THE OTHER PERSON.
HEY, ASAHARU MAMIYA.

DON'T YOU WANT TO BRING YUUKA MAMIYA BACK TO LIFE?

SHE'S RIGHT.
TIGHTEN
THAT IS MY OBJECTIVE.
I WILL...
...BRING HER BACK TO LIFE.

SHOVE
WHOOSH
THUNK

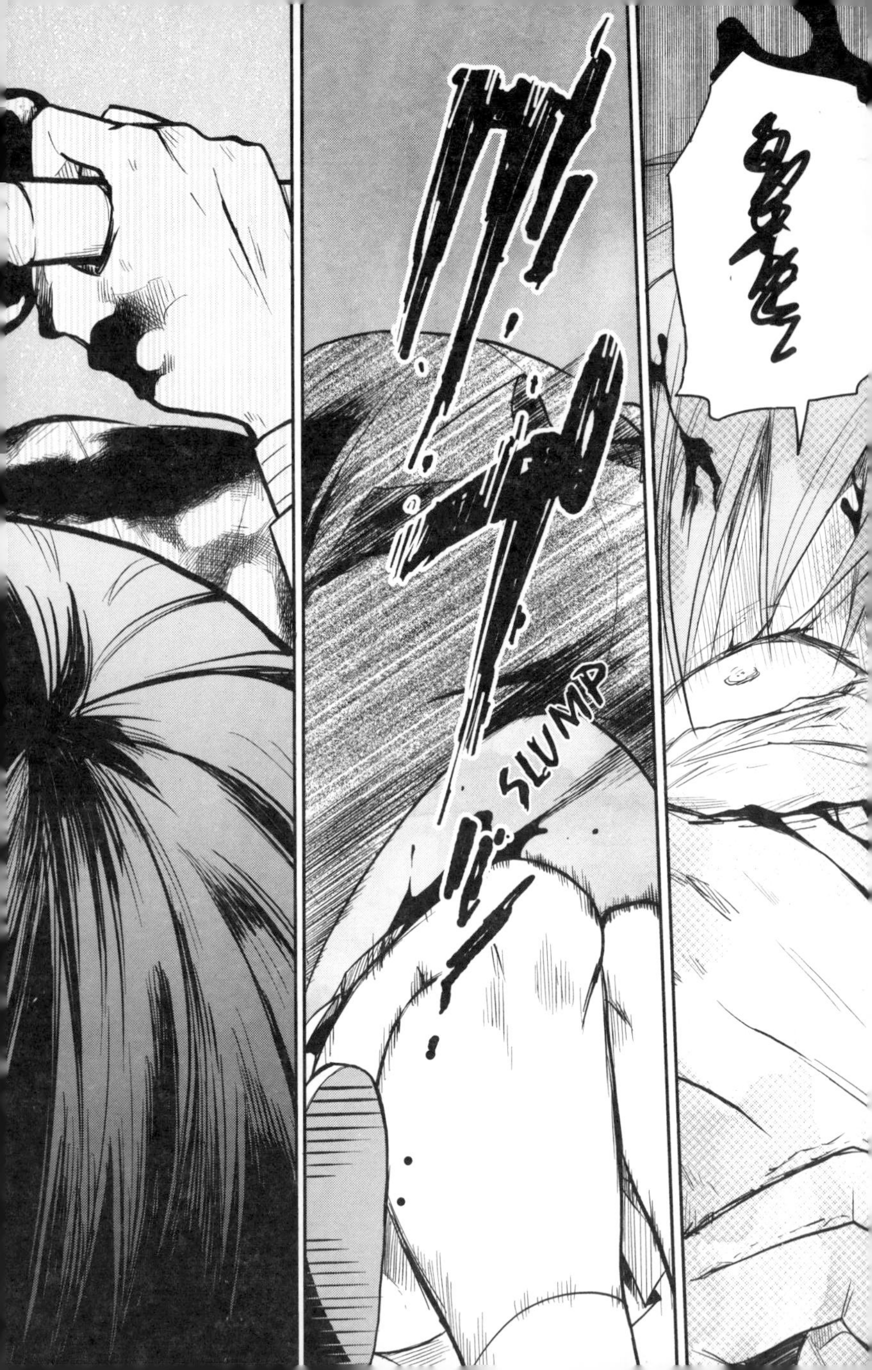
SLUMP

I'M SORRY, BUT...
...IT'S YOUR FAULT. YOU GOT WHAT YOU DESERVED.

CONGRATULATIONS.
パチパチ
CLAP
CLAP
EVEN THOUGH YOU KEEP KILLING THEM SO VIOLENTLY.
YOU HESITATED, BUT YOU DID A WONDERFUL JOB.

YOU WANT A HIGH FIVE AS A REWARD?
HURRY UP AND REVIVE YUUKA!

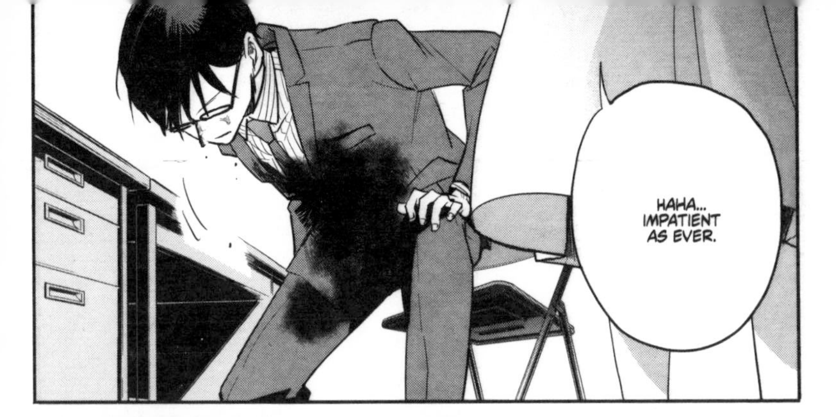
HAHA... IMPATIENT AS EVER.

HEY, ASAHARU.
DO YOU REMEMBER THE RULES?
OF COURSE I DO. THEY WERE PRETTY SIMPLE.

IF I KILL THE CULPRIT, YUUKA COMES BACK TO LIFE.

THAT'S RIGHT.
IF YOU KILL THE PERSON RESPONSIBLE...
...FOR DRIVING HER TO KILL HERSELF.

FLAP
EASY, RIGHT?

HEY!
COME ON, HURRY UP!
HOWEVER...

IT'S A REAL SHAME. YOU FAILED.
CRACK
CRACK
HUH...?
crack

CRASH

WHOOSH
WHAT...?!

COME ON.

TIME
TO START
OVER.
GRIN

ENDROLL BACK

Loop.3 Truth

HEY!

IT'S A REAL SHAME, BUT SHIMIZU ISN'T THE ONE RESPONSIBLE.
THAT'S WHY YOU HAVE TO START FROM SCRATCH.
AND, ADDITIONALLY, YOU GET A PENALTY.
WHAA

BADUMP
...
SLAM
!!

PLIP
ポタ
PLIP
タ..

WA...
WAIT A MINUTE!

SHIMIZU...
...BULLIED YUUKA.

AND SHE WAS ALSO THE ONE THAT CUT UP THE TENNIS SHOES.
...

WHO DID YOU SAY DID THAT?
ハ?...
SIGH
?
I TOLD YOU THAT SHIMIZU...
!!

THAT'S RIGHT. AKANE SHIMIZU WAS THE ONE THAT CUT UP YUUKA MAMIYA'S TENNIS SHOES.
WERE YOU THE ONE THAT CUT UP THE TENNIS SHOES?
NOT THE TENNIS SHOES OF THE THIRD YEARS.
YOUR QUESTION WAS TOO VAGUE.

ALSO, THE WIN CONDITION IS...
...KILLING THE PERSON THAT WAS RESPONSIBLE FOR DRIVING YUUKA MAMIYA TO HER DEATH.

THERE'S NO DOUBT THAT AKANE SHIMIZU CONTRIBUTED TO THE BULLYING, BUT SHE WASN'T THE CULPRIT.

YOU MADE A MISTAKE WHEN YOU DECIDED THAT THE ONE RESPONSIBLE FOR EVERYTHING WAS AKANE SHIMIZU.
IF YOU KEEP ON GOING LIKE THIS, I CAN ALREADY PREDICT HOW EVERYTHING'S GOING TO END.

I STILL HAVE A CHANCE.
GRIP
I CAN'T KEEP LOSING THESE CHANCES, OR LOSING MORE TIME THAN NECESSARY.
I NEED TO THINK ABOUT WHAT I CAN DO NOW!!
LET ME CHOOSE MY NEXT ABILITIES.

SWIPE
WHATEVER YOU SAY.
WHICH ONES WILL YOU CHOOSE THIS TIME?
Force Co
Object Re
The replica will disapp
Time Master: Able to sto
Teleportation: Able to tele
Lockpicker: Can
Temporal Re
Mate

THEY ALL SEEM USEFUL, BUT THEY ALL HAVE THEIR DRAWBACKS.
MEMORY SEEK'S DESCRIPTION IS REALLY VAGUE.

I NEED ONE THAT WILL PROVIDE ME WITH PRECISE INFORMATION.
すっ
POINT
FOR THAT...
Force Confession: Force a
Object Replication: Copy an object th
ピタ
BEEP
HEY.
Time Master

IF I USE THIS ABILITY TO COPY A CELL PHONE...
ARE THE SAME FILES AND DATA SHARED BETWEEN THEM?

THAT'S RIGHT.

Copy
Asaharu
You free tomorrow?
Sent
Original
Asaharu
You free tomorrow?
WHEN A MESSAGE IS SENT TO THE ORIGINAL CELL PHONE, A COPY OF IT WILL GO TO THE REPLICA.

AND IF YOU RESPOND USING THE REPLICA, IT'LL ALSO SHOW UP IN THE ORIGINAL PHONE.
BUT...

BE CAREFUL, BECAUSE THEY AREN'T ON THE SAME SCREEN IN REAL TIME.
FOR EXAMPLE, IF YOU OPEN THE CAMERA APP ON THE REPLICA...
...THAT WON'T MAKE THE ORIGINAL PHONE'S CAMERA APP OPEN AT THE SAME TIME.

I UNDERSTAND...
IN THAT CASE...

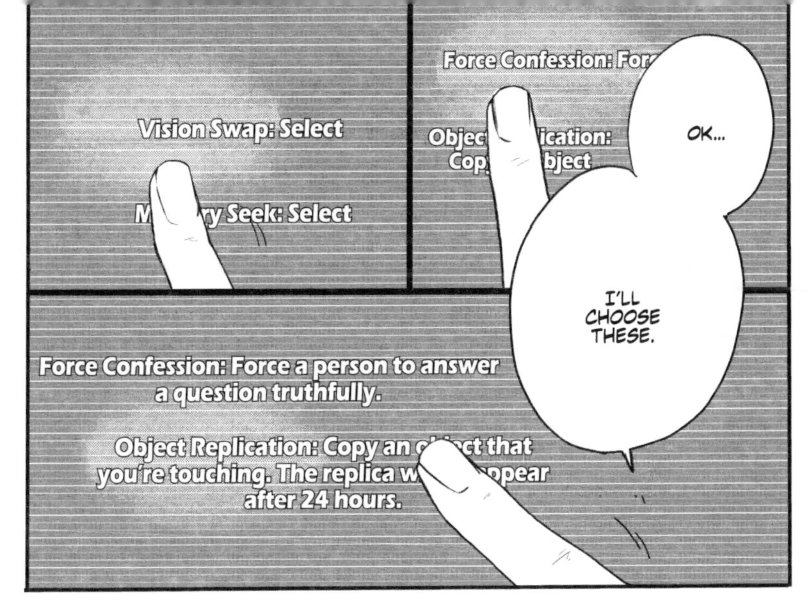
Vision Swap: Select
ry Seek: Select
Force Confession: For
Object lication:
Cop bject
OK...
I'LL CHOOSE THESE.
Force Confession: Force a person to answer a question truthfully.
Object Replication: Copy an o ect that you're touching. The replica w ppear after 24 hours.

GOOD!

SNAP
LET'S START THE THIRD LOOP!

THAT'S WHY, UNTIL MR. FUKUDA RETURNS...
MR. HIYOSHI WILL TAKE OVER THE CLASS FROM TODAY ONWARDS.
WELL, PLEASE INTRODUCE YOURSELF.
YES.
MY NAME IS ASAHARU HIYOSHI, AND I'LL BE THE SUBSTITUTE TEACHER FROM NOW ON.
I WILL TEACH MR. FUKUDA'S JAPANESE HISTORY CLASS.
THE REASON FOR MY LAST TWO FAILURES IS CLEAR.
I'VE JUMPED TO CONCLUSIONS TOO MUCH.
I HOPE WE ALL GET ALONG.

I HAVE THREE MONTHS.
I'LL DO THIS STEP BY STEP.

I NEED TO BE CAUTIOUS AND, ABOVE ALL, PATIENT, TO FIND THE CULPRIT.
AND THEN...

YUUKA WILL
COME BACK
TO LIFE!

I NEED TO WALK AROUND THE SCHOOL NOW...
...AND RUN INTO HIMENO SAEKI, WHO'S LOOKING FOR SOMETHING.
WHEN I LEAVE THE SECOND YEARS' FOURTH PERIOD, I'LL GO EAT...
...AND I'LL HAVE TO LISTEN TO THE TEACHER WHO WON'T ALLOW ME TO ESCAPE.
AFTER CLASSES END...
I WON'T GO TO THE RECORDS ROOM. I'LL GO TO THE TRASH AREA INSTEAD.
THERE I'LL RUN INTO AKANE SHIMIZU AND THE BASKETBALL GIRLS.

THEY'RE RUNNING AWAY FROM ME.
I CAN'T STOP THEM FROM THROWING AWAY YUUKA'S TENNIS SHOES.

THEY HAVEN'T STOPPED BOTHERING YUUKA IN CLASS EVER SINCE.
Waste

AND THAT'S WHY SHE STARTED TO AVOID US.
I UNDERSTAND. THANK YOU.
UP TO NOW, EVERYTHING'S REMAINED THE SAME.

NOW, THE REAL BATTLE STARTS.

RECORDS
SEPTEMBER 2, 9:00 AM.

WERE YOU THE ONES THAT THREW AWAY YUUKA'S TENNIS SHOES?
...

LISTEN... BOTH OF YOU GOT ALONG DURING YOUR FIRST YEAR.
YOU WERE FRIENDS, WEREN'T YOU?

DO WHATEVER YOU WANT.
YOU CAN TALK ABOUT IT DURING THE TEACHERS' MEETING TOO.
I'M SURE THAT THEY CAN PUT A STOP TO THIS AND FIX EVERYTHING.

BUT I'D LIKE FOR YOU TO RESOLVE IT AMONGST YOUR-SELVES...
EITHER WAY...
IT'S YOUR FAULT THAT THIS IS HAPPENING, BECAUSE YOU KNOW ABOUT IT BUT HAVEN'T DONE ANYTHING ABOUT IT.
CLENCH

IN THE END, NO ONE EVER CARES ABOUT US.

...

TEACHER, YOU ASKED ME IF I WAS A FRIEND OF YUUKA'S...
EVEN I...
VRRR

!

OH

I HAVE TO GO.

DO WHATEVER YOU WANT ABOUT THE TENNIS SHOES THING.
I DON'T CARE IF YOU CALL MY PARENTS EITHER.

ガタッ
STAND
HUH?
WAIT!

...
SLAM

WHY DON'T YOU JUST LET HER GO?
WHAT DOES IT MATTER ANYWAY?
NO...

IF I DEDICATE MYSELF TO HELPING THEM ONE BY ONE...
I'M CERTAIN THAT THE TRUE CULPRIT WILL COME TO LIGHT.

THAT'S WHY I HAVE TO FOCUS ON MAKING EVERYONE GET ALONG AGAIN.
CLENCH

Basketball girls
Akane, can you come?
You know if it's important to Yuuka?
She loves that keychain.
That's true! She always has it.
Great!

YOU REALLY LIKE KEYCHAINS?

HERE, I'LL GIVE YOU...
...THIS.
WOW! WHAT AN UGLY LITTLE BEAR.

WHAT?! BUT IT'S SUPER CUTE!
IT'S HIDEOUS.
AT LEAST IT MAKES YOU LAUGH!
SORRY, IT'S JUST THAT THE PRESENT'S MADE ME REALLY HAPPY.
IF I LOOK AT IT CLOSELY, IT REALLY IS CUTE.
TWIST
TWIST

THANK YOU SO MUCH...
...AKANE!
THAT THING THAT HAPPENED WITH THE THIRD YEARS' TENNIS SHOES WAS SO TYPICALLY YUUKA.
YOU THINK SHE WENT CRAZY BECAUSE SHE WASN'T ABLE TO PLAY?

WHAT AN AWFUL PERSONALITY.
SHE THINKS SHE'S BETTER THAN US.
ちら
GLANCE
SHE DOESN'T HAVE IT ON HER BAG.
IT LOOKS LIKE SHE DOESN'T HAVE IT ANYMORE.

WELL?

CAN YOU LET ME KNOW WHAT ALL THAT WAS ABOUT?

I'M GETTING EVERYTHING READY SO THAT SHIMIZU STOPS BULLYING YUUKA.
BUT I HAVEN'T SEEN ANYTHING SUSPICIOUS.

ALTHOUGH IT'S OBVIOUS THAT YOU'RE ALSO WORRIED ABOUT...
...HER.
IT'S JUST THAT WHEN I WAS TALKING WITH SHIMIZU, I SAW THAT THINGS WEREN'T GOING SO WELL FOR HER.

THAT'S WHY, IF I CAN MAKE HER CHANGE, I MIGHT BE ABLE TO UNDERSTAND WHAT'S GOING ON.
THAT'S ALL.
I THOUGHT HE WAS DOING IT JUST BECAUSE HE WAS A GOOD PERSON.
HERE SHE COMES...

ス
TAP
ガッ
BAM
!!

SLAM
OOPS.
CLACK
OW...
SORRY!
OH...

ARE YOU OK?

...

HERE.

YOU DROPPED THIS.
THANKS...

HEY, SHIMIZU.

IF YOU EVER NEED ANY HELP, JUST SAY THE WORD.

I'M HERE FOR EVERYONE.

I'LL BE THERE TO HELP YOU WHENEVER YOU NEED ME.

YOU GOT IGNORED.

JUST HER HEARING IT IS ENOUGH.
ALSO...

I GOT WHAT I WANTED.

OBJECT REPLICATION

WHAT ARE YOU THINKING ABOUT DOING WITH THAT?
SHUT UP...
...AND WATCH.

CREAK
*BASKET-BALL CLUB
STOP.
YOU HURT ME.

UGH!

THE WAY YOU'RE LAYING THERE DISGUSTS ME.
THANKS TO YOU, I THINK I HURT MYSELF.

IT WON'T HURT YOU TO GIVE IT TO ME. YOU HAVE A BUNCH OF THEM.

LOOK...

THE TEACHER'S CALLING YOU.
YOU HAVE TO GO NOW...

TANIZAKI'S ANNOYING WHEN HE GETS WORKED UP.
BUT THE OTHER DAY YOU...

T-THANKS...
AKANE.
...
TIE
TURN
SLAM

EVERYONE!

LET'S STOP FOR TODAY.
YUUKA, PICK EVERYTHING UP. WE HAVE THINGS TO DO.
THE FIRST YEARS CAN LEAVE TOO.

HEY, YOU GUYS...
IT'S FINE, TEACHER.

THEY'RE ALL BUSY. I CAN DO IT BY MYSELF.
MAMIYA...
SEE? THERE'S NO PROBLEM HERE. SHE SAID IT HERSELF.
YOU'LL DO IT TOMORROW, OK?
WHATEVER YOU SAY!
SIGH

"YOU WERE FRIENDS, WEREN'T YOU?"
!
DON'T WORRY... I CAN DO IT BY MYSELF.

IT'S OK.
IT'S NORMAL TO CLEAN UP AFTER YOURSELF.
HUH...?
ゴソ…
RUSTLE

ガサ
RUSTLE
LOOKS LIKE NAMI AND THE OTHERS STOLE SOMETHING FROM HER.
ガサ
RUSTLE

BEEP

Bring her to the empty classroom on the third floor. And don't let her escape.
Tell her that I'll give back what I stole from her.
NOW THEY'RE THREATENING ME, INDIRECTLY.

YUUKA, NAMI WANTS YOU TO COME WITH ME.
THEY'RE GOING TO GIVE BACK WHAT THEY STOLE FROM YOU.
OH--
OK.

SLIDE

!

THE TEACHER'S GOING TO PRETEND HE DIDN'T SEE US, HUH...

WHAT DID THEY TAKE FROM YOU THIS TIME?

A-A KEYCHAIN...
OH, BECAUSE I TOLD THEM ABOUT IT.

WELL, YOU DO HAVE A LOT OF THEM. ONE LESS WOULDN'T MAKE A DIFFERENCE.
YOU DON'T KNOW WHAT THEY'LL DO TO YOU IF YOU GO. WHY NOT IGNORE THEM AND GO HOME?

NO, THAT KEYCHAIN'S WAY TOO IMPORTANT TO ME TO LET THEM KEEP IT.
ALSO...

...IF I RUN AWAY, WHO KNOWS WHAT THEY'D DO TO YOU.
WHO CARES...

YOU'RE FINALLY HERE.
TOOK YOU LONG ENOUGH, AKANE.

SORRY...

YUUKA.
SIT OVER HERE.

UMM... I WANT YOU TO GIVE ME BACK MY KEYCHAIN...

I'LL GIVE IT BACK IF YOU DO WHAT I SAY, OK?
BANG

SUMIRE, LOCK THE DOOR.
OK.
I TOLD HER SHE SHOULD HAVE RUN AWAY.

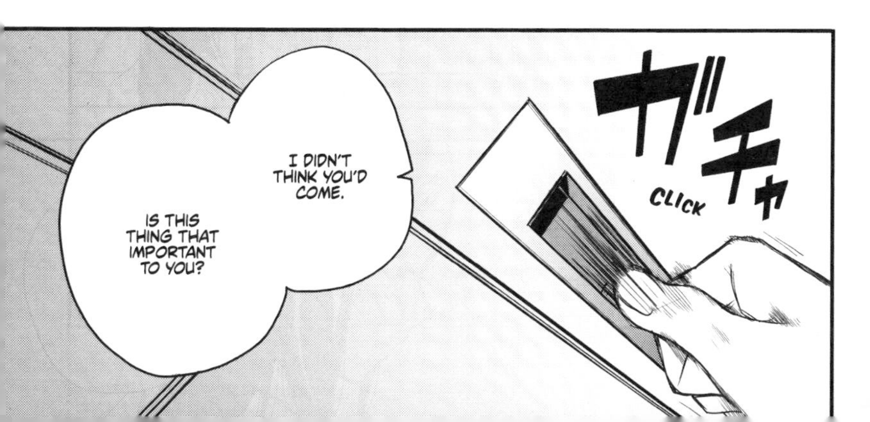
ガチャ
CLICK
I DIDN'T THINK YOU'D COME.
IS THIS THING THAT IMPORTANT TO YOU?

チャ
JANGLE

THAT'S...

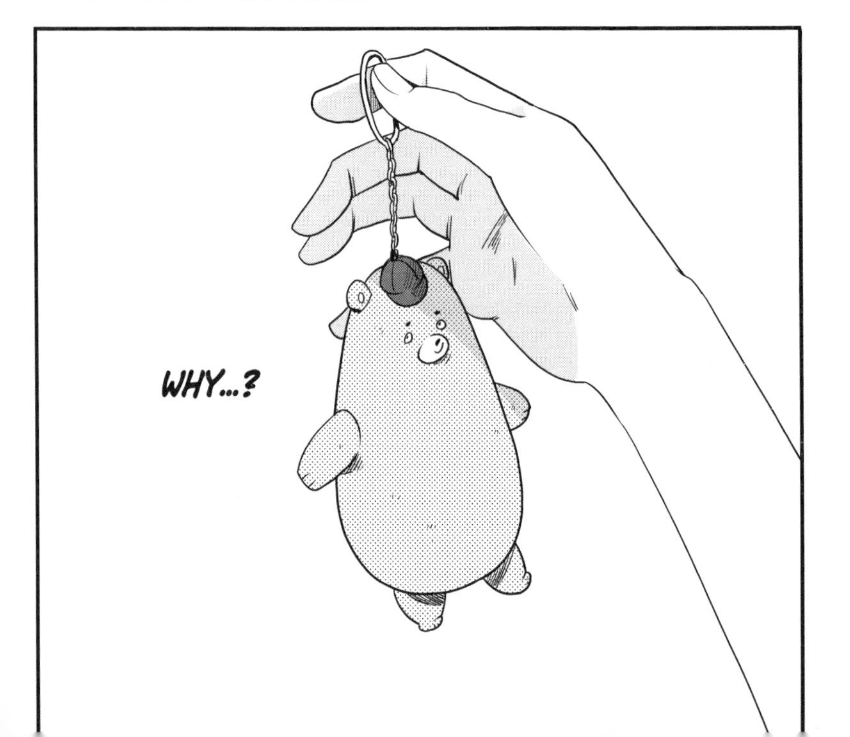
WHY...?

IF SHE NEVER HAD IT ON HER BAG...
PLEASE GIVE IT BACK!
FINE.
ON ONE CONDITION.

IF YOU PROMISE ME THAT YOU'LL QUIT THE BASKETBALL CLUB, I'LL GIVE IT BACK.
HUH?

IT'S BECAUSE YOU'RE A NUISANCE.
ALSO, YOU PLANNING ON STEPPING ONTO THE COURT WITH YOUR STREET SHOES?
BUT THAT'S...
I DON'T WANT TO HEAR ANY EXCUSES!

I'M TELLING YOU THAT YOU'RE A NUISANCE.
IF YOU DON'T QUIT...

I'LL LIGHT IT ON FIRE.

STOP!
ドカ
BAM
I TOLD YOU ALREADY...
ガリ
SLAM
...IF YOU QUIT, I'LL GIVE IT BACK.

I HATE THAT YOU'RE SO STUBBORN.
WHY DO YOU LIKE THIS DISGUSTING THING?

SO?
WHAT ARE YOU GONNA DO?

ALRIGHT, YOU WIN. I'LL QUIT THE CLUB.
PLEASE, GIVE IT BACK!

REALLY?
FINALLY!
...

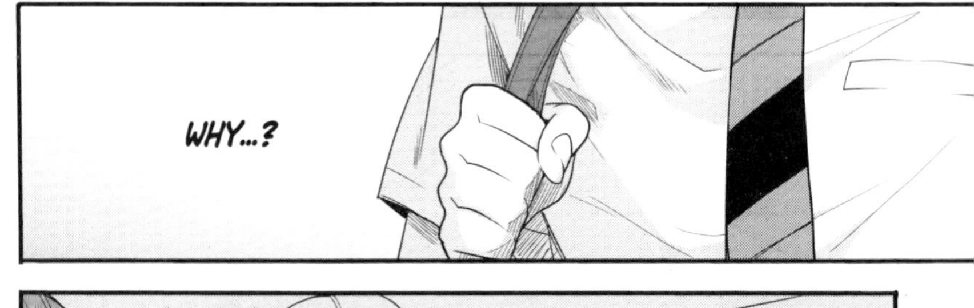
WHY...?

THAT KEYCHAIN IS A USELESS TRINKET.
WHY LET EVERYTHING GET TO THIS POINT?

WHAT A JOKE.
HERE.
ヒュッ
WHOOSH

WHY...
...DON'T YOU EVER HAVE IT ON YOUR BAG?

I THOUGHT THAT IF I PUT IT ON MY BAG, YOU'D START TO TREAT ME BADLY TOO.
WHAT...
...DID YOU SAY?

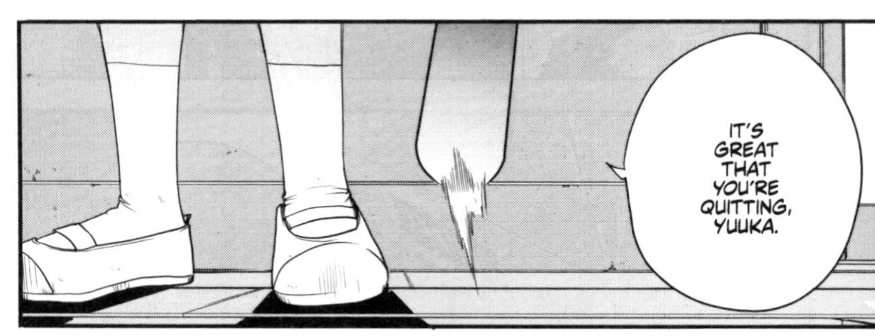
IT'S GREAT THAT YOU'RE QUITTING, YUUKA.

NOW...
YOU DON'T NEED YOUR RIGHT ARM, DO YOU?

HUH?

NAMI, WHAT ARE YOU SAYING?!
IT WILL LOOK WEIRD IF YOU QUIT OUT OF THE BLUE, SO THERE NEEDS TO BE A REASON.

IF YOUR ARM IS BROKEN THEN YOU WON'T BE ABLE TO THROW THE BALL.
ISN'T THAT WONDERFUL?

YOU'RE CRAZY!
YOU DON'T HAVE TO GO THAT FAR!
WHOOSH
WHAT?!
BLINK
NOW YOU PRETEND TO BE THE GOOD GIRL?
OR DO YOU WANT TO QUIT THE CLUB TOO?

...

CALM DOWN, AKANE. STAY THERE AND WATCH.
す LOWER
I'VE ALWAYS WANTED TO KNOW WHAT IT FEELS LIKE...
...TO HIT SOMEONE WITH A BAT.
ME TOO!

YOU...
...READY?
THRASH
GRAB

SLAM

DON'T MOVE.
STOMP
STO--
STOP...

"THAT KEYCHAIN'S WAY TOO IMPORTANT TO ME TO LET THEM KEEP IT."
"IF I RUN AWAY, WHO KNOWS WHAT THEY'LL DO TO YOU."
"I THOUGHT THAT IF I PUT IT ON MY BAG, YOU'D START TO TREAT ME BADLY TOO."

ALRIGHT, HERE I GO!
STOP!!
どっ
BAM
SLIP

SLAM
WHAT?! NAMI!!

AKANE...

I'M SORRY...
I'M SORRY, YUUKA...

YOU'VE ALWAYS...
...MADE ME A PART OF YOUR LIFE.
I WAS JUST WORRIED ABOUT MYSELF...
I DIDN'T SAY ANYTHING BACK THEN...
...EVEN THOUGH WE WERE FRIENDS.

FORGIVE ME...
AKANE...
OUCH...
STOP, NAMI.
YOU CAN STILL WALK AWAY FROM ALL THIS.
YOU'RE STILL...
TAP
ARE YOU STUPID?!
す
RAISE

I'VE HAD ENOUGH OF YOU, AKANE.
WHY DON'T YOU QUIT THE CLUB TOO?
GRIP
SOMEONE...
"IF YOU EVER NEED ANY HELP, JUST SAY THE WORD."

TEACHER...

TEACHER, HELP ME...
TEACHER...!

LUNGE

CRASH

IT WAS LOCKED.

LUCKILY, I WAS ABLE TO BREAK THE WINDOW.
カチャ
CLICK
TEACHER...?
DIDN'T I SAY THAT I'D HELP YOU?
TAP TAP

GOOD JOB, SHIMIZU.
ポー
PAT

じわ
SLIDE
ふぁ
SLUMP

AND NOW...

THIS IS BULLYING, ANY WAY YOU LOOK AT IT.

HA HA.
WHAT ARE YOU TALKING ABOUT?

DOESN'T ENTERING THROUGH THE WINDOW SHOW THAT YOU HAVE A REAL SCREW LOOSE?
THAT'S RIGHT! WE WERE JUST TALKING.

OH, SURE... COME ON.

YOU HAVE NO PROOF THAT WE WERE BOTHERING HER.
THAT'S JUST AN IDEA THAT POPPED INTO YOUR HEAD. YOU'RE EXAGGERATING THINGS.

YOU WANT PROOF? I HAVE IT.

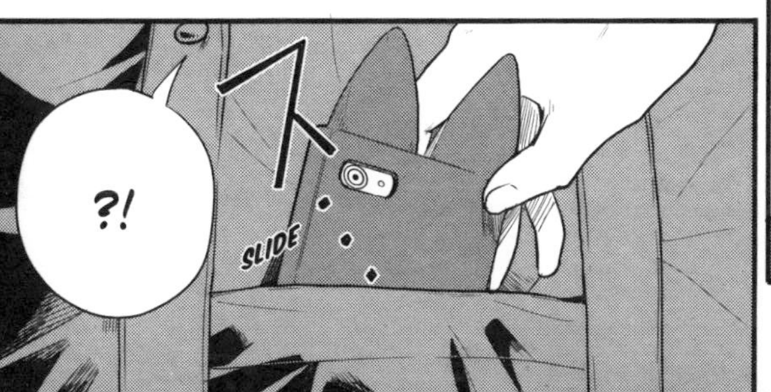
SLIDE
?!

IT'S GREAT THAT YOU'RE QUITTING, YUUKA.
YOU DON'T NEED YOUR RIGHT ARM, DO YOU?
HUH?
NAMI, WHAT ARE YOU SAYING?!
IT WILL LOOK WEIRD IF YOU QUIT OUT OF THE BLUE, SO THERE NEEDS TO BE A REASON.

IF YOUR ARM IS BROKEN THEN YOU WON'T BE ABLE TO THROW THE BALL.
ISN'T THAT WONDERFUL?
YOU'RE CRAZY! YOU DON'T HAVE TO GO THAT FAR!
Voice Recording
04

YOU...
...RECORDED IT?

I ASKED SHIMIZU TO DO ME THE FAVOR OF RECORDING THE CONVERSATION.
RIGHT?
HUH?
OH, RIGHT...

OF COURSE I DIDN'T ASK HER TO DO ANYTHING.

WHAT I USED WAS...
...THE REPLICA OF HER PHONE.

IF I USE THIS ABILITY TO COPY A CELL PHONE...
ARE THE SAME FILES AND DATA SHARED BETWEEN THEM?
THAT'S RIGHT.
IF I COPY A CELL PHONE, BOTH OF THEM SHARE THEIR DATA.
IN THAT CASE...
ALL THEIR PERSONAL INFORMATION AND MESSAGES ARE COPIED TOO.

IF I COULD CONNECT THE ORIGINAL TO A COMPUTER AND COPY ITS CONTENTS, THEN I'D BE ABLE TO LOOK THROUGH EVERYTHING QUICKLY.
SO IF I COPY THE INFORMATION FROM THE CELL PHONE REPLICA ONTO MY COMPUTER...

WHERE IS IT GOING TO HAPPEN?
YUUKA... NAMI WANTS YOU TO COME WITH ME.
THEY'RE GOING TO GIVE BACK WHAT THEY STOLE FROM YOU.
I CAN LOOK THROUGH ALL OF THE ORIGINAL CELL PHONE'S INFORMATION TOO.
O-OK.

IF I DO THAT, THEN I CAN RECORD THEIR CONVERSATION.
YOU'RE CRAZY! YOU DON'T HAVE TO GO THAT FAR!
I RECORDED THE WHOLE CONVERSATION FROM THE BEGINNING.

SO NOW THAT WE'RE ALL ON THE SAME PAGE...
WHY DON'T YOU COME WITH ME FOR A MOMENT TO TALK?
RECORDS
WHAT DO YOU WANT TO TALK ABOUT?
WHY NOT CALL OUR PARENTS OR CALL FOR A TEACHER MEETING? I DON'T CARE!
HEY, NAMI...

THAT'S RIGHT. DON'T GET AHEAD OF YOURSELF.
THE LEADER OF THE BULLYING SEEMS TO BE HER, NAMI IIJIMA.
I SHOULD USE IT ON HER.

THIS TIME, I CAN'T MAKE ANY MISTAKES.
FORCE CONFESSION

IIJIMA...
WHY DO YOU BULLY MAMIYA SO BLATANTLY?
FLASH
す

BECAUSE...

...SHE ASKED ME TO HERSELF.

WHAT...
...DID YOU SAY?

Endroll Back Vol. 1 - End

ENDROLL BACK

ENDROLL BACK

ENDROLL BACK

Thank you for buying the first volume of Endroll Back! I'm the author, Kantetsu.

This work is my first foray into the genre of time loops and special abilities. I've enjoyed writing a story that's different from all I've done until now, thanks in great part to the impressive art and compositions of my artist partner, Nakazato. I still get excited every time I read the scene where the angel appears in the first chapter.

I also want to thank Mikami, my editor, for her precise advice and her constant help.

The story has just begun. Who is the one responsible for Yuuka's death at the end of the first volume? Will Asaharu be able to discover the truth? I hope you enjoy the next chapters.

See you in the next volume.

Kantetsu.

DESIGNS
ASAHARU HIYOSHI
BINGO!
DEAD
DEAD
BECAUSE ASAHARU MAMIYA HAS TO TRANSFORM INTO ASAHARU HIYOSHI, I CREATED THESE THREE DRAFTS. I LOVE THEM ALL.
TOO HANDSOME.
WASN'T MUCH OF A CHANGE.

EXTRA
ILLUSTRATION:
SORA KAWASAKI
AZUMI KODA
NOZOMI TEKAMI
SEMI MAIKAWA
AYA YABANE
EDITOR:
TAKEHIKO MIKAMI
THANK YOU SO MUCH FOR YOUR HELP!
THANK YOU FOR BUYING ENDROLL BACK! I TRULY APPRECIATE YOUR SUPPORT. I'M NAKAZATO, THE PERSON IN CHARGE OF THE ARTWORK. ENDROLL BACK IS A TYPE OF STORY THAT I'VE NEVER DRAWN BEFORE. IT WAS REFRESHING AND FUN TO WORK ON THE ILLUSTRATIONS FOR THIS MANGA. I ALSO LEARNED A LOT DURING THE PROCESS. ALTHOUGH MY DRAWING STYLE MIGHT NOT BE PERFECT, I FEEL LIKE I'M IMPROVING BIT BY BIT.
I HOPE YOU KEEP SUPPORTING THIS SERIES!

WAIT!
YOU'RE GOING THE WRONG WAY!

TRADITIONAL JAPANESE MANGA IS READ FROM RIGHT TO LEFT! MAKE SURE YOU FOLLOW THE DIRECTIONS BELOW WHEN READING PAGES, PANELS, BALLOONS AND SOUND EFFECTS!

EDITOR IN CHIEF: **Matias Timarchi**
SENIOR EDITOR: **Lysa Hawkins**
EDITOR: **Matias Mir**
ASSISTANT EDITORS: **Martin Casanova & Clara Bartolozzi**
SALES & OPERATIONS: **Danielle Ward**
TRANSLATION: **Gustavo Alvarez & Ignacio Gonzalez**
LETTERING: **Marina Leon**
PR & SOCIAL MEDIA: **Rodrigo Molina**

ENDROLL BACK

ENDROLL BACK VOL. 1